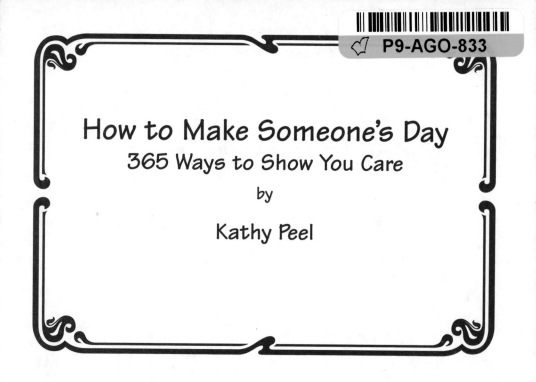

How to Make Someone's Day
365 Ways to Show You Care

by

Kathy Peel

How to Make Someone's Day: 365 Ways to Show You Care
Copyright © 1994 by Kathy Peel

Scripture quotations used in this book are from the following sources:

The Amplified Bible (AMP). Copyright © 1965 Zondervan Publishing House. Used by permission.
The Holy Bible, New International Version (NIV). Copyright © 1973, 1978, 1984 International Bible Society. Used by permission of Zondervan Bible Publishers.
The Living Bible (TLB), copyright 1971 by Tyndale House Publishers, Wheaton, Illinois.
The New King James Version (NKJV). Copyright © 1979, 1980, 1982, Thomas Nelson, Inc., Publisher.

Library of Congress Cataloging-in-Publication Data

Peel, Kathy, 1951–
     How to make someone's day : 365 ways to show you care / Kathy Peel
        p.   cm.—(Quick me ups)
     ISBN 0-8499-3574-1
     1. Kindness.   I. Title.   II. Series.
  BJ1533.K5P44   1994
  177' .7—dc20   94–5467
                                                                    CIP

Printed in the United States of America.

"Scatter joy!"—Ralph Waldo Emerson.

When we sincerely do something for or give something to someone else, we are blessed twice. Genuine giving always gives joy to the giver as well as the receiver. In our busy lives, when we take time out to give a little joy to someone else, we get it back even more. We get the good feeling of having done something for someone else. We can be pleased that we've eased someone else's path. And we often find that in giving a kind word, a small treat, an outing to someone else, we've also stopped to give the same thing to ourselves.

Scattering joy doesn't have to be a grand gesture or an expensive gift. A smile and a few kind words can mean just as much, or more. A friend shared with me that once when she was under intense stress from her family and career, an older woman came up to her outside the grocery store. The woman appeared from her accent to be a Russian immigrant. She looked at my friend and said, "So tired, you look so tired. You take care." My friend burst into tears, because she indeed was tired, but mostly because some other human being noticed and took the care to mention it. By this "random act of kindness," a stranger had scattered joy.

In order to scatter joy, we don't necessarily have to be joyful ourselves. Often, joy comes on the backstroke. We don't obtain it by chasing after our own good, our own happiness, our own fulfillment. Much of the time joy comes to us when we give joy to others—our families, our friends, and strangers.

When we give joy to others, God's grace gives us back all we give. People who take time for others find themselves taking time for themselves, and in building the connections between themselves and others find that others take time for them. This business of giving joy is a win/win and keep-on-winning situation.

I am grateful to my friend H. Jackson Brown who, when he wrote *Life's Little Instruction Book*, intended that his son Adam would learn a few things about living. Little did Jackson know that he would teach millions of the rest of us a lot about living. In our busy world, we need I-can-at-least-do-this-one-little-thing ideas. In the tradition of his books, I hope *How to Make Someone's Day* helps you scatter seeds of joy.

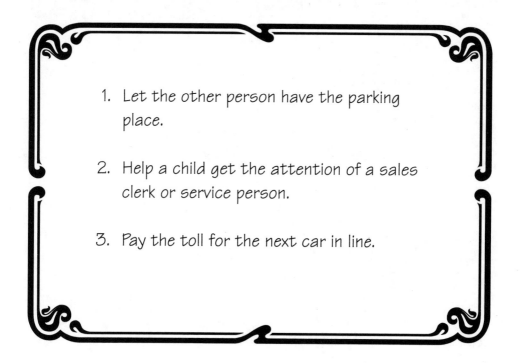

1. Let the other person have the parking place.

2. Help a child get the attention of a sales clerk or service person.

3. Pay the toll for the next car in line.

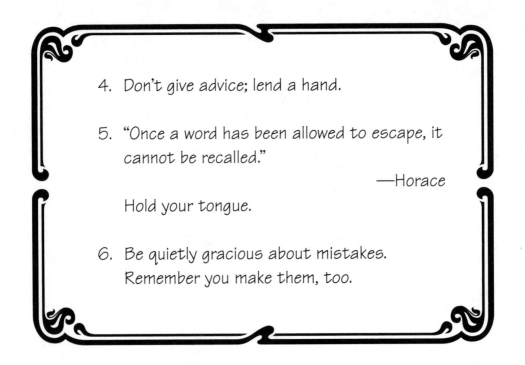

4. Don't give advice; lend a hand.

5. "Once a word has been allowed to escape, it cannot be recalled."

    —Horace

    Hold your tongue.

6. Be quietly gracious about mistakes. Remember you make them, too.

7. Welcome new neighbors with a basket of paper goods and lunch fixings. Also give them a list of your favorite shops and services in the area.

8. Finish a task for someone who's tired.

9. Let a mother with young children go ahead of you in line at a public restroom.

10. Give a stranger directions, or lead them to the road they're looking for.

11. "Everyone should keep a fair-sized cemetery in which to bury the faults of his friends."
—Henry Ward Beecher
Do your friend the favor of not harping on his faults.

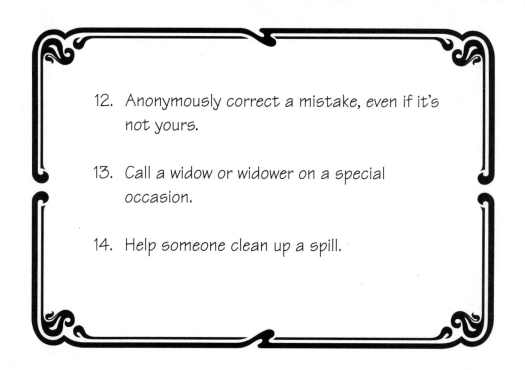

12. Anonymously correct a mistake, even if it's not yours.

13. Call a widow or widower on a special occasion.

14. Help someone clean up a spill.

15. "I can live for two months on one good compliment."

—Mark Twain

Compliment a friend specifically on something he did or how he looks.

16. Sit with a friend in a hospital waiting room.

17. Tutor a child in a subject you're particularly good at. Volunteer through your school or local social agency.

18. Offer to deliver a friend to the airport for an early morning flight.

19. Turn off the TV and offer to listen when you think someone wants to talk.

20. Drop a penny where someone will find it.

21. Show interest in your friend's work. Ask questions like, "What do you like best about your job?" and "What is your greatest challenge at work?"

22. Serve breakfast in bed to a loved one who's been under stress.

23. Praise a job well done, even if it's something you expected that person to do.

24. "Do not use a hatchet to remove a fly from your friend's forehead." —Chinese Proverb
Be gentle in your efforts to help.

25. Plan a fun outing for someone who's had a hard week.

26. Take time to talk to a child. Get down on his level, look him in the eye, and speak his language.

27. Visit an elderly neighbor.

28. Subtly tell a friend she has lipstick on her teeth, or her slip is showing.

29. Meet someone more than halfway.

30. Take a photograph of a friend, put it in a frame, and send it to her.

31. When a friend is due home from a lengthy trip, leave milk, orange juice, and muffins in her refrigerator.

32. "See to it that you really do love each other warmly, with all your hearts."—I Peter 1:22 (TLB) Don't be shy about telling someone you love them.

33. Put some loose change between sofa pillows. When a child discovers it say, "Finders keepers, losers weepers."

34. Don't eat extravagantly in front of a friend who's dieting.

35. Move to the right on the freeway to let the person who's in a hurry pass you, no matter how inconsiderate he or she seems.

36. Stand up for someone else's rights.

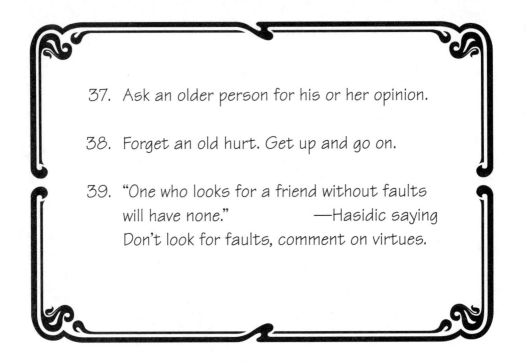

37. Ask an older person for his or her opinion.

38. Forget an old hurt. Get up and go on.

39. "One who looks for a friend without faults
    will have none."   —Hasidic saying
    Don't look for faults, comment on virtues.

40. Let someone with just a few items go ahead of you at the grocery store.

41. Host a surprise party for someone dear.

42. Cheer for a friend's home team.

43. Pick up litter in a neighbor's yard.

44. Stand in for a friend who doesn't have time to go to a meeting.

45. Be a gracious receiver when somone gives you a gift, even if it's something you don't like.

46. "And the Lord restored the fortunes of Job when he prayed for his friends."

—Job 42:10 (NIV)

To pray for a friend is also to pray for ourselves.

47. Offer to clean a sick friend's home or apartment.

48. Stand in front of a mirror with someone who's had a hard day. Make faces at each other and laugh.

49. Give a toast to someone.

50. Write down a meaningful poem or a quote and stick it in someone's lunchbox.

51. Search out a long-lost friend.

52. Sit with a friend and enjoy silence together.

53. "A joy shared is a joy doubled." —Goethe
Share your joy with your friends.

54. Spray a little perfume on your paper when you write a letter to someone special.

55. Ask someone if they'd like a backrub.

56. Help someone with a stroller up some stairs.

57. When you're on a vacation, pick up extra brochures, maps, and information to share with a friend who might want to travel there too.

58. Let a child beat you in a game.

59. Adopt a grandparent.

60. Put money in a stranger's expired parking meter.

61. Keep a secret secret.

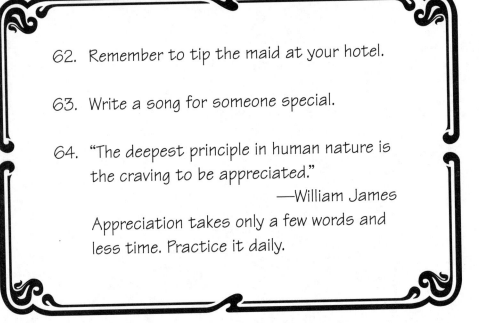

62. Remember to tip the maid at your hotel.

63. Write a song for someone special.

64. "The deepest principle in human nature is the craving to be appreciated."

—William James

Appreciation takes only a few words and less time. Practice it daily.

65. Send flowers for no reason except to say you care.

66. Write a thank-you note to your child's teacher.

67. Say thanks with a word or a small gift to someone who faithfully performs a behind-the-scenes job.

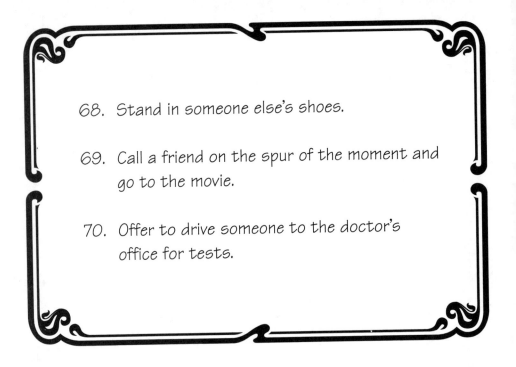

68. Stand in someone else's shoes.

69. Call a friend on the spur of the moment and go to the movie.

70. Offer to drive someone to the doctor's office for tests.

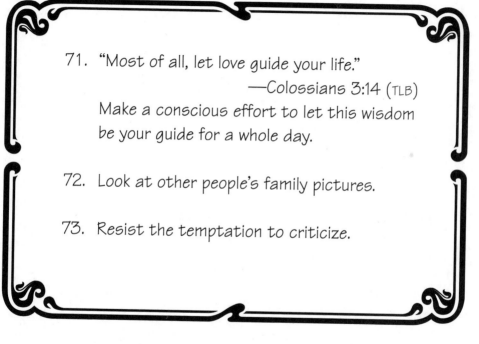

71. "Most of all, let love guide your life."

—Colossians 3:14 (TLB)

Make a conscious effort to let this wisdom be your guide for a whole day.

72. Look at other people's family pictures.

73. Resist the temptation to criticize.

74. Help a friend overcome a fear by talking with her or maybe offering to take a class together.

75. Go out of your way to help—even if you'll be late.

76. Help a friend rearrange furniture and decorate a room.

77. Pay a debt for someone.

78. "A friend is a present you give yourself."
                              —Robert Louis Stevenson
    Take a friend to lunch as a present
    to both of you.

79. Ask a mother with small children if you can return her shopping cart from the parking lot for her.

80. Clip an interesting magazine article, and mail it with a note to someone who might enjoy it.

81. Go out of your way to put in a good word for someone to the appropriate person.

82. Draw a warm bath for a family member who's had a hard day. Fluff and warm his towel in the dryer.

83. Do a chore for your spouse so he or she can sleep in.

84. Offer to help anyone who looks like they might need it—with a door, reaching an elevator button, or with a package.

85. Watch a craftsperson at work. Compliment his or her skills.

86. Create a cartoon and give it to someone who could use a laugh.

87. Put flowers on a coworker's desk.

88. Thank your children for doing their regular chores.

89. "To let friendship die away by negligence . . . is to voluntarily throw away one of the greatest comforts of this weary pilgrimage."

—Samuel Johnson

Contact a friend you've neglected.

90. Plan a getaway weekend so you and your spouse can have some uninterrupted time to share your deepest thoughts and dreams and renew your friendship.

91. "A friend loves at all times."

—Proverbs 17:17(NIV)

Be loving even at times when you're correcting a child or complaining to a store clerk.

92. Has a friend been dragging his feet or procrastinating about a project? Ask what you can do to help him get started.

93. When you cook in quantity for your own family, make an extra casserole to give away.

94. "If we advance through life and do not make friends, we shall soon find ourselves alone. We must keep our friendships in constant repair." —Samuel Johnson

The phone is a great tool to repair a friendship. Pick it up today.

95. If you have a friend who's made a fool of himself, let him know he hasn't done a permanent job.

96. Give the person ahead of you in line the cents he or she needs to make correct change.

97. "Be kind and compassionate to one another, tenderhearted, forgiving each other, just as in Christ God forgave you."

—Ephesians 4:32 (NIV)

Ask a friend for forgiveness.

98. Do a mundane chore with a friend. It will make the task more pleasant.

99. "It is one of the blessings of old friends that you can afford to be stupid with them."
—Ralph Waldo Emerson

Admit to a friend that you didn't know something. Ask for an explanation.

100. One's own name is sweet music to the ear. Say a person's name often when speaking to them.

101. Encourage a friend to be her best. Help her visualize her potential.

102. "A pleasant companion reduces the length of a journey." —Cyrus
If a friend is in crisis or sick, offer to provide regular help over the long haul, maybe dinner once a week.

103. Give up your seat on a bus or train.

104. Ask if you can pick up a friend's out-of-town relatives at the airport when they arrive for a wedding or funeral.

105. Say yes when kids come to your door and ask if you'd like to buy candy or cookies to raise funds for their school or team.

106. "If you love someone you will be loyal to them no matter what the cost."
—I Corinthians 13:7 (TLB)

Give up some work time for a friend in need.

107. Treat your family like they're company.

108. Respect a friend's privacy. Offer support, but don't press for confidences.

109. It's the friend you can call at 4 A.M. who's really a friend. Let someone know you're always there no matter what time they need you.

110. "The first duty of love is to listen."

—Paul Tillich

Make sure your friend knows that a duty is not necessarily a burden.

111. Encourage a child by sharing your story of learning to ride a bike or whatever.

112. Take a sick friend a pot of chicken soup and two or three new magazines.

113. Make a special certificate of achievement to celebrate someone's success.

114. If you've neglected a friend because of a full calendar, don't remind her of how busy you are. Simply do the best you can to stay in touch, even if it's a short phone call.

115. "The most precious of all possessions is a wise and loyal friend." —Herodotus
Treat a friend like the precious thing he is.

116. Schedule a special coffee break for someone at the office. Bring pretty mugs, cinnamon sticks to stir your coffee, and some muffins from home.

117. Ask an elderly person to tell you a story from his or her youth.

118. When someone lives her life in a way that you admire and want to emulate, tell her.

119. "Friendship with oneself is all-important because without it one cannot be friends with anyone else in the world."

—Eleanor Roosevelt

Be a friend to yourself.

120. Buy a book on cassette for a friend who doesn't have time to read.

121. Take photographs of people and things around you and send them to a friend who has moved away.

122. Challenge someone to do the things he's always dreamed of.

123. Ask an elderly neighbor if you can bring her anything from the store when you go.

124. Overtip a waitress who looks like she's had a hard day.

125. Give someone who looks tired your place in a long line.

126. Share a good book you've just finished with a friend. Get together and talk about it when she's through.

127. Invite a friend to eat dinner and spend the night when her husband is out of town.

128. Take dinner to a parent who's holding down the fort while the other one travels.

129. "The future is purchased by the present."
    —Samuel Johnson
    Do something thoughtful for someone
    you'd like to build a relationship with.

130. When someone shares a difficult situation
    with you over the telephone, ask if you can
    pray for him or her right then and there.

131. Pick wildflowers and make a pretty arrangement for someone.

132. Keep small presents and wrapping supplies on hand. This makes it easy to give a gift on a whim.

133. "Two are better than one; If one falls down, his friend can help him up."

—Ecclesiastes 4:9-10 (NKJV)

Call a friend who's in trouble just to let her know you're thinking of her.

134. Don't worry if you want to honor someone and you're short on money. When you give someone your presence, you're giving the most.

135. Clinging to your own importance is the quickest way to lose it. Make a habit of seeing others as more important than yourself.

136. Don't wait for a special occasion to give someone a present. Out-of-the-blue gifts add joy to any moment.

137. Ask a friend to share a positive childhood memory.

138. Time spent together cements a relationship. When passing through cities where you have friends, call or write ahead so you can get together, even if it's for only a few minutes.

139.   Keep an envelope in a drawer with money especially designated to be used to make fun memories with people you care about.

140.   Take your address book and stamps with you on trips. Send postcards with warm messages to those you love.

141. Sit and watch a friend do something she's good at. Ask her how she feels when she's expressing her gifts and talents at the task.

142. Write a warm note of appreciation and stick it in someone's briefcase before a business trip.

143. "What do we live for, if it is not to make life less difficult for each other."

—George Eliot

Make your life worth living.

144. Paper-clip pages in clothing catalogs and mark items that you think look like a friend. Give her the catalog with a note that you were thinking of her.

145. Invite someone to take dancing lessons with you.

146. "I thank my God upon every remembrance of you." —Philippians 1:3 (NKJV)
Pray for a friend when he or she comes to mind.

147. Sometimes just saying the words "I love you" is not enough—we need to be shown. Hug somebody who needs it.

148. When a friend goes on a business trip to make a big proposal, send an encouraging message by fax to her hotel.

149. Give someone you love an Eskimo kiss by rubbing noses.

150. Write "I love you" or "Welcome Home" on your driveway or sidewalk to welcome a family member home.

151. "Friendships are glued together with little kindnesses." —Mercia Tweedale
Practice them daily.

152. Hang red paper hearts in a child's doorway at his or her eye level for a morning greeting.

153. Send a friend a pressed flower for a bookmark just to say "thank you."

154. Write out a prayer for a friend and send it to him or her in the mail.

155. "If you can dream it, you can do it."

—Walt Disney

Encourage friends to step out and follow their dreams.

156. Throw your neighbors' paper up on their porch.

157. Write a poem about someone and give it to him or her.

158. Send an inspiring cassette to someone who has a long commute.

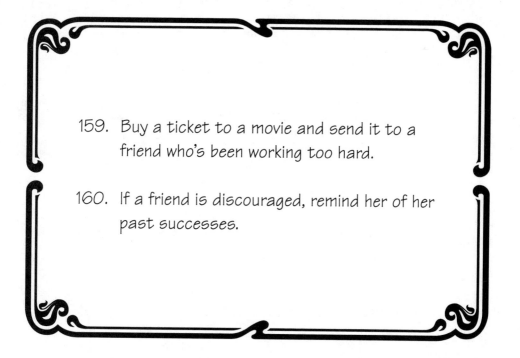

159. Buy a ticket to a movie and send it to a friend who's been working too hard.

160. If a friend is discouraged, remind her of her past successes.

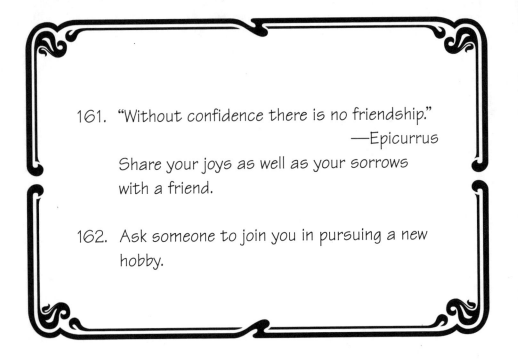

161. "Without confidence there is no friendship."
—Epicurrus

Share your joys as well as your sorrows
with a friend.

162. Ask someone to join you in pursuing a new
hobby.

163. Offer a coworker a lift to work. Focus your conversation on positive topics rather than problems.

164. Go for a drive through the countryside with someone special.

165. Put an encouraging note in your spouse's coat pocket.

166. Offer to exercise with a friend who's trying to lose weight.

167. "Love keeps no record of wrongs."
—I Corinthians 13:5 (NIV)
Burn your list of grievances toward a friend.

168. Give someone the gift of inspirational music. Music is the language of the soul.

169. Ask someone to join a fellowship or support group with you.

170. If a friend is depressed, help him or her start a project. Working together can be healing.

171. "Do to others as you would have them do to you."
—Luke 6:31 (NIV)
This familiar advice can't be followed too often.

172. Spend some time outside with someone special to you. Crush leaves under your feet, lie down in a field of wildflowers, climb a mountain, watch a sunset, or sit by a lake.

173. Remind children of their greatness. Say something like, "If someone lined up all the seven-year-olds in the world and told me to pick one, I'd pick you."

174. Send a humorous card with a loving message to your spouse's office.

175. Be actively interested in someone else's world.

176. If a friend fails, don't give a lecture or sermon.

177. "The ornaments of a house are the friends who frequent it." —Ralph Waldo Emerson
Open your home often to friends and family.

178. Help a friend recover from a bad day by role-playing with exaggeration the day's events.

179. "We should behave to our friends as we would wish our friends to behave toward us."
—Aristotle

When you're angry with a friend, speak kindly in a non-threatening way.

180. Go with an animal lover to a pet show.

181. Rent a recreational vehicle or camper and ask someone special to go on a weekend getaway.

182. Work on a religious holiday for someone of a different faith.

183. Bring a good joke to work.

184. Help a friend reframe a problem into an opportunity.

185. Get your car washed by kids raising money for a church mission trip.

186. When you meet a coworker for a crack-of-dawn work session, bring warm muffins and special coffee in a thermos.

187. Buy a blank book for a friend who's expressed an interest in starting a journal.

188. Smile. You'll bring joy to others when they see you. Plus, psychological tests prove that we feel better when we smile.

189. Begin a collection for a child. Add to it periodically.

190. "Nothing, so long as I am in my senses, would I match with the joy that a friend may bring."　　　　　　—Horace
Let a friend know how much joy she brings you.

191. Give a teddy bear to a friend—of any age.

192. "For we are God's workmanship, created in Christ Jesus to do good works, which God prepared in advance for us to do."
—Ephesians 2:10 (NIV)

Tell someone she is a unique piece of art created by the greatest Master.

193. When you visit a museum, buy a set of postcards and bring the museum home to a friend.

194. Next time you read a good paperback book, buy an extra copy and give it to a friend.

195. Make a special scrapbook of photographs and memorabilia for someone you cherish.

196. Don't throw away old catalogs and magazines. Offer them to a friend who would enjoy them.

197. Fill an emergency basket for the office with lotion, stockings, a small sewing kit, packages of cocoa and chicken broth, cologne, breath spray, pain reliever, and antacids. Invite coworkers to help themselves.

198. Call a busy friend and set a date to meet for an early breakfast to catch up.

199. "So long as we love we serve; so long as we are loved by others, I would almost say that we are indispensable; and no man is useless while he has a friend."

—Robert Louis Stevenson

When you're feeling useless, do something nice for a friend.

200. Place little notes, "I love you," "I miss you," inside a loved one's suitcase when he or she goes on a trip.

201. Deliver more than you promise—in every relationship. You, as well as your friends, will be richer for it.

202. Give a foot massage to a loved one who's had a long day.

203. "One main test of our dealings with the world is whether the men and women we associate with are better or worse for it."
—George MacDonald
Make someone better today.

204. Be easy to please. If you don't care where you eat dinner, allow your friend to choose.

205. Play golf or tennis with someone who's just learning, even if you're more proficient.

206. Be patient with a person who's having a hard time catching on to something.

207. Don't demand credit. Give someone else the spotlight.

208. Value others' freedom.

209. When a friend has a new baby, give a present to her older children so they'll feel special.

210. Pack a picnic lunch and take someone special to a surprise location.

211. Have a cookie-baking evening. Make several kinds to take to the office or send to a college student.

212. Ask a loved one to make a wish list for Christmas and birthday gifts.

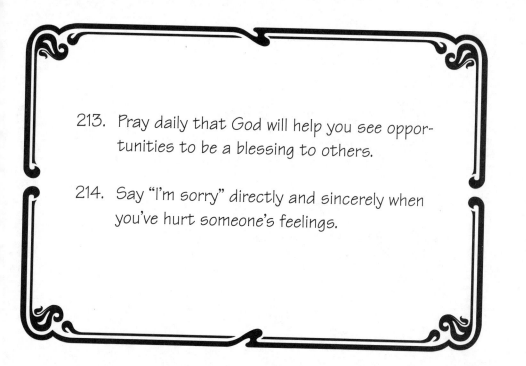

213. Pray daily that God will help you see opportunities to be a blessing to others.

214. Say "I'm sorry" directly and sincerely when you've hurt someone's feelings.

215. "To ease another's heartache is to forget one's own." —Abraham Lincoln
Visit a bereaved person just to say you care.

216. Let a friend cry on your shoulder.

217. "Treat your friends as you do your pictures, and place them in their best light."

—Jennie Jerome Churchill

And then tell them how good they look.

218. Never say "I told you so" to anyone, at any time.

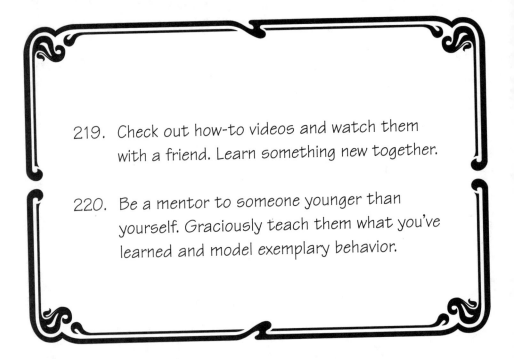

219. Check out how-to videos and watch them with a friend. Learn something new together.

220. Be a mentor to someone younger than yourself. Graciously teach them what you've learned and model exemplary behavior.

221. Start a book club with coworkers. Invite them to read the same book, then get together at lunch and discuss what you read.

222. "As iron sharpens iron, so one man sharpens another." —Proverbs 27:17 (NIV) Whom do you sharpen?

223. Organize a trip to take with friends you don't get to see as often as you'd like.

224. To the best of your ability, be a person of your word.

225. Being a friend to someone is a high calling. You can influence her character for good or bad.

226. Try to remember first names and something about every person you meet. When you meet again, you'll show that you care.

227. Try to look your best every day for those around you. This will make their world more pleasant.

228. "Once a word has been allowed to escape, it cannot be recalled." —Horace
When you have a conflict with a friend, ask God to help you choose your words carefully.

229. Help someone you care about reach a personal goal.

230. Tell someone you like that you accept and respect your differences.

231. "Sometimes when I consider what tremendous consequences come from little things . . . I am tempted to say there are no little things."

—Bruce Barton

Do a little something for someone you care about.

232. Write an encouraging note to a coworker who's facing a demanding assignment that day.

233. God handpicked you to be his representative to the world. Do acts of kindness with this in mind.

234. "I am only one; but I am one, I cannot do everything, but I can do something; I will not refuse to do the something I can do."

—Helen Keller

Don't refuse to do something you can for a friend.

235. Don't expect a friend to be perfect.
You're not.

236. "It is a rough road that leads to the heights of greatness."

—Lucius Annaeus Seneca

When searching for intimacy produces pain, which it often does, remember intimacy is a great endeavor.

237. Ask yourself how a friend would describe you. What could you change that might make your relationship stronger?

238. Play inspirational music for a friend who's upset. Good music soothes our souls and brings peace to our minds.

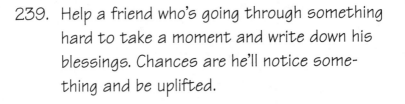

239. Help a friend who's going through something hard to take a moment and write down his blessings. Chances are he'll notice something and be uplifted.

240. "Nobody, who has not been in the interior of a family, can say what the difficulties of any individual of that family may be."

—Jane Austen

Offer solace, not criticism of others' crises.

241. Help a friend brainstorm solutions to her problem. Be careful not to impose your own.

242. Express your confidence to a coworker that they can do a challenging job.

243. Care for your friends, but don't overwhelm them.

244. Send a dinner guest home with a bag full of homemade chocolate-chip cookies.

245. Keep notes of your friends' interests. Talk about things they enjoy.

246. "A friend is a person with whom I may be sincere; before whom I may think out loud."
—Ralph Waldo Emerson
Share a new idea with a friend.

247. Send a telegram to say "Congratulations" to someone special.

248. Greet a new member at church. Ask about his or her interests. Make them feel at home.

249. Start a tradition of doing a little extra something for someone you love on a particular day—besides the obvious occasions—each year.
Celebrate your relationship.

250. Treat a friend with a gift certificate to a favorite restaurant.

251. Respond, don't react. Be careful not to say something you'll regret later.

252. Invite the neighborhood children over for a tea party.

253. Put canned goods into your grocery store's food-barrel drive.

254. Invite a single person to Thanksgiving dinner or dinner anytime.

255. "A friend can tell you things you don't want to tell yourself." —Frances Ward Weller
Be accountable with a friend to help each other be your best.

256. Make a donation to a friend's favorite charity to celebrate his promotion.

257. "Faithful are the wounds of a friend."
—Proverbs 27:6 (NKJV)
If you think a friend's criticism of you is unfounded, ask her to help you see your blind spot.

258. Give someone the gift of confidence. Encourage and compliment an area in which she feels inadequate.

259. If you borrow someone's car, return it with a full tank of gas.

260. Greet everyone you meet today with a smile.

261. "The most I can do for my friend is simply to be his friend." —Henry David Thoreau Send this quote on a pretty card to a friend who's feeling down.

262. Ask a single friend to ride with you and your spouse to a party or reception so she won't have to walk in by herself.

263. Call your family before you leave work and ask if there is anything you can pick up on your way home.

264. Offer to let a friend borrow a dress or accessory for a special occasion so she won't have to buy a new one.

265. Control the tone and volume of your voice when you're angry with someone. Yelling at another human being—unless there's a dangerous emergency—is demeaning and disrespectful.

266. Ask a neighbor who's extra busy if you can take her turn driving the kids' carpool. Give her the day off.

267. Invite a close friend to shop for bathing suits together. Make a difficult task an occasion for laughter.

268. Give a friend who's feeling down about herself a day-of-beauty gift. She might enjoy a facial, manicure, pedicure, or makeup consultation.

269. Dress up and give someone a personal singing telegram to lift his or her spirits.

270. "No one is useless in this world who lightens the burden of anyone else."

—Charles Dickens

Make yourself useful by listening to a friend's woes.

271. Leave a message on a friend's answering machine simply to let him know you're thinking about him.

272. Call if you're going to be late.

273. Teach your children to hug Dad or Mom when he or she comes home from a long day.

274. When someone tells a joke you've already heard, laugh anyway, and resist giving away the punch line.

275. Answer the phone and take messages for someone who's tired.

276. When you know your spouse has a busy day, get up early and lay out his or her clothes, or arrange toiletry items conveniently, or do anything else that will help him or her get out the door with less stress.

277. Frame a greeting card that a friend sent you that meant a lot. Give it back with a warm message as a token of your friendship.

278. Send a tape-recorded love letter to someone special.

279. Play a friend's favorite music while you're working on a project together.

280. Stop by an ice-cream shop and pick up something scrumptious to take to a coworker who's under the pile.

281. Ask a person you care deeply about, "How can I bring joy to your day?"

282. "Happy is the house that shepherds a friend."
    —Ralph Waldo Emerson
    Make your home a place of rest and welcome.

283. Never criticize another person in public.

284. Bake a friend's favorite dessert and surprise her with it.

285. If someone offers to help you do a task, be appreciative. Don't criticize the way they do it if they don't meet your standards.

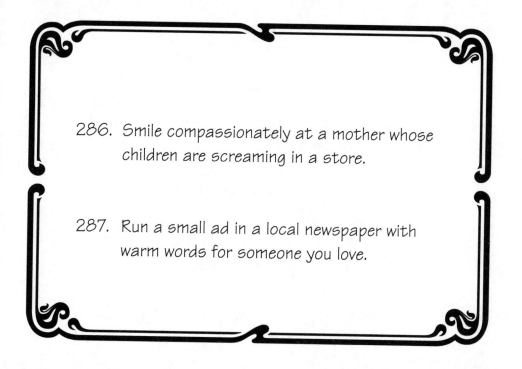

286. Smile compassionately at a mother whose children are screaming in a store.

287. Run a small ad in a local newspaper with warm words for someone you love.

288. Hug a friend after you've worked through a disagreement.

289. Write "I love you" on a fogged window or mirror.

290. Bring a tall glass of iced tea or lemonade to someone who's working outside.

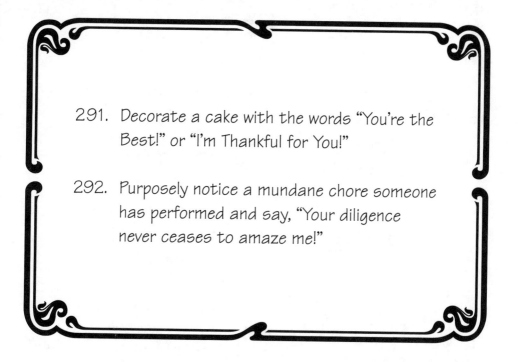

291. Decorate a cake with the words "You're the Best!" or "I'm Thankful for You!"

292. Purposely notice a mundane chore someone has performed and say, "Your diligence never ceases to amaze me!"

293. Tell a friend, "I really enjoy your smile!"

294. Take a minute and write a thank-you note to your child's teacher.

295. Design special letterhead for a friend on your computer, such as "Mary White— World's Best Friend," then write her a note.

296. Say "I really admire you" to someone who exhibits character traits worth emulating, especially a young person.

297. A healthy relationship is built between people who understand that self-worth is more important than net worth.

298. The heaviest load any person can carry is a grudge. Drop some baggage today.

299. "As you travel through life my brother, to have happiness untold, keep your eye upon the doughnut, and not upon the hole."
                                        —Author unknown
Let this principle rule your relationships.

300. Drag your neighbor's empty garbage cans from the curb back to their usual location.

301. Take a friend's child birthday or Christmas shopping for her. Help the child choose an appropriate gift.

302. Attend a lecture with a friend. Talk about what you learned over coffee afterwards.

303. When you come to an impasse in a relation-
      ship, break through with honest talking;
      don't break down with harsh words.

304. Remind a friend she is a human becoming,
      not just a human being.

305. Money spent making memories with someone you care about is a wise investment
that brings many happy returns.

306. Don't let a hard experience with a friend
paralyze your relationship. Take a small
step toward something you think you
cannot do.

307. When someone you care about is hurting, remember you can't do everything, but at least you can do something.

308. "A friend should bear his friend's infirmities."
                                                    —Shakespeare

Let someone know you empathize.

309. Turn a stumbling block in a friendship into a steppingstone.

310. Showing up five minutes early for an appointment shows you respect someone else's time and life.

311. Start your day in a positive way so you can be a blessing to others. Wake up one hour earlier and spend it alone reading inspirational material and praying.

312. Help a friend see his cup as half full instead of half empty.

313. "It is in the character of very few men to honor without envy a friend who has prospered."   —Aeschylus

Rejoice with a friend over his success.

314. Kidnap someone you care about who's had a hard week. Use a bandanna as a blindfold and travel in a roundabout way to her favorite restaurant.

315. Play Monopoly™ with a child and make sure he gets Boardwalk and Park Place.

316. Browse together at a flea market looking for vintage magazines. Laugh with a friend about the fashions of your youth.

317. Reward extra effort at the office by crowning someone King or Queen for the day.

318. Make a family videotape and send it to Grandma and Grandpa.

319. Invite a friend over to your home and have an old-fashioned taffy pull.

320. Have a fix-it day to show that you care about your children's belongings.

321. Tell someone you'd enjoy hearing them play a musical instrument—even if they haven't practiced in a while.

322. When you see kids with a lemonade stand, buy one for yourself and for everyone who passes while you're standing there.

323. Send a long-distance friend a few postcards, some stamps, and a new pen. Tell her you'd enjoy hearing about what's going on in her life.

324. Clip the coupons of a friend's favorite products and give them to her.

325. Plan a "Guest of Honor" dinner for someone who's under a lot of pressure. Dress up, get out your best china, and eat by candlelight.

326. Take someone's hand, look them in the eye and say, "You're a very valuable person. It is a privilege to know you."

327. "The best mirror is an old friend."

—George Herbert

Honor your friend by asking for advice.

328. Thank a salesclerk for good service.

329. Volunteer to work in a soup kitchen for the homeless. This is a great thing to do with an older child.

330. "Fate chooses our relatives, we choose our friends."　　　　—Jacques Delille

Tell a friend why you chose her.

331. Fill your spouse's car with gas.

332. Call a friend long distance just to say you're thinking of her.

333. "We cannot tell the precise moment when friendship is formed. As in filling a vessel drop by drop, there is at last a drop which makes it run over; so in a series of kindnesses there is at last one which makes the heart run over." —James Boswell

Do kind deeds every day.

334. Bring treats to an evening meeting without being asked.

335. Offer to entertain a small child for a bit during a long flight for a parent traveling alone.

336. "Without friends no one would choose to live, though he had all other goods."

—Aristotle

Throw a party for your friends to let them know how much you appreciate them.

337. Thank your parents for things they did years ago when you were little, even if you've done it before.

338. "Greater love hath no one than this, that he lay down his life for his friends."

—John 15:13 (NIV)

Donate blood for a friend who's having surgery.

339. Be sure to wave "thanks" when somebody lets you into traffic.

340. Leave someplace, like an airplane bathroom or a rented cottage, cleaner than you found it.

341. Offer to keep a friend's children when her usual sitter cancels.

342. Resist the urge to pat your pregnant friend's stomach.

343. When a friend buys a new computer, offer to teach him how to use it.

344. Surprise friends by having pizzas delivered to their house on moving day.

345. Stop and give a jump-start to someone whose car has a dead battery.

346. Videotape a television program you know a friend will miss because of a business meeting.

347. Offer to give up your seat on an airplane so a family can sit together.

348. Don't complain about gaining five pounds to a friend who's gained twenty-five.

349. When you see a family or group taking pictures of each other, offer to take one of the whole group.

350. Smile at police officers. Thank them for being on the job.

351. Offer to pick up and return library books for someone who is homebound.

352. Ask neighbors if you can feed their pet or water their yard when they're out of town.

353. Write down birthdays of all family members and friends. Stock up on cards and stamps.

354. Turn off the TV when someone wants to talk to you.

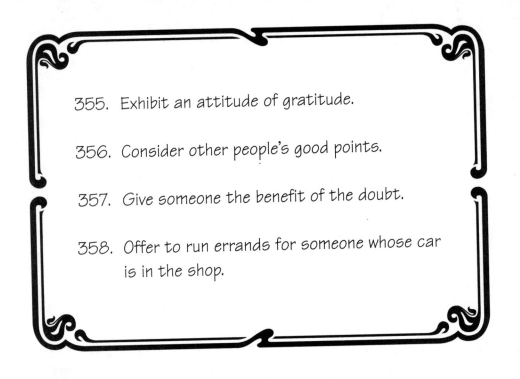

355. Exhibit an attitude of gratitude.

356. Consider other people's good points.

357. Give someone the benefit of the doubt.

358. Offer to run errands for someone whose car
     is in the shop.

359. Ask a friend if she's lost weight.

360. Read a book to a friend's child when you're visiting with the parents.

361. Frame a special picture or document for a friend's office.

362. Be a "there you are" person, not a "here I am" person.

363. "Friendship is unnecessary, like philosophy, like art. . . . It has no survival value; rather it is one of those things that gives value to survival." —C. S. Lewis

364. Return something you've borrowed with a small thank-you gift.

365. Compliment a stranger on her hairstyle or outfit.